A Night in Vienna

A Novella By

Betty Ann Hoehn

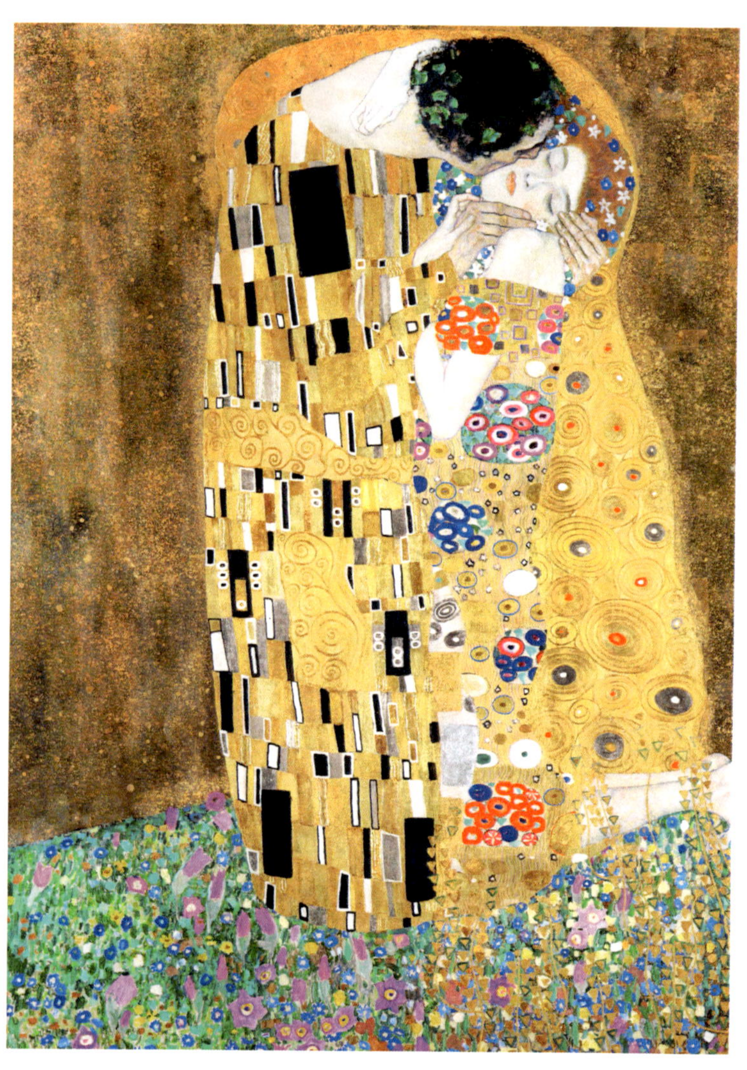

Gustav Klimt: The Kiss. Oil on canvas. 1907-1908

Chapter One

The Art Gallery

On this winter day, Vienna is alive with celebration. The entire city wears a festive look. Christmas trees adorn vibrant, music-filled streets. Holiday lights shine from store windows, casting a warm glow on the faces of people walking past. Joyful chatter permeates the wintry air.

Far from the bustling streets and outdoor markets, the atmosphere is very different for one woman lost in her thoughts, feeling at home inside the elegant Belvedere Gallery. The art gallery is quiet, the mood enchanting.

Staring out the window, Emma is mesmerized by the pristine landscape covered in blankets of snow. She contemplates the stillness outside, the grey atmosphere, the snow flurries that come and go. The snow-covered lawn and sky have become one, a dividing line between the two nearly impossible to distinguish.

Emma's love affair with Vienna extends to virtually everything about the Austrian capital city on the Danube River. As an art historian and a classical pianist, she has always gravitated to its music and art, the exquisite architecture, and the wonderful people—really, everything about this European cultural center that brought Mozart and Beethoven to this world.

This isn't her first visit to the Belvedere. Emma had been here many times, walking down the halls, studying the artwork that grace the walls of this 18th-century, Baroque-style Vienna jewel, one of the oldest museums on the planet. She has perused its many galleries time and time again, noting the paintbrush strokes and special techniques that define each artist and exemplify an art movement.

But this visit feels different somehow, though she doesn't know why. The winter atmosphere may be putting her in a contemplative mood.

Stepping back from the window, she walks across the stylish interior to study portraits by early 20th-century Austrian artist Gustav Klimt. She pauses at one of her favorite paintings and focuses her attention on the life-size couple on its canvas. Painted in 1908, *The Kiss* draws Emma in. Even after many years she is still hypnotized by this evocative painting. At the age of 68, she continues to be a hopeless romantic. To her, *The Kiss* embodies a true, *pure* expression of love—a mystical blend of carnal and spiritual love.

Lost in her world, she suddenly realizes how eerily quiet the museum has become. How long has she been standing here, reflecting on this work of art? As she continues to gaze at the lovers on the canvas, she senses someone walking up and pausing next to her. Her body freezes from being startled, her heart palpitates, both involuntarily.

Emma turns to see who it is, and she almost blushes when her eyes meet his. She does not recognize the tall man with a full head of dark blonde-grayish hair, piercing blue eyes, chiseled face, and a somewhat intense demeanor, but he certainly captures her attention. For a moment her breath is taken away. A long pause that feels like an eternity stretches between them, and in that silence, it's evident the two feel the pull of some kind of connection, the type that only kindred spirits tend to experience.

The striking gentleman smiles and reaches out to initiate a handshake. His eyes steal a quick glance at her long, copper hair with wisps of gray before settling warmly on her hazel eyes. As she grasps his hand, she feels an electric spark of chemistry pass between them.

"Hello, I'm Poul," he introduces himself in a quiet, velvety voice. "I am from Denmark."

"Hi, I'm Emma," she responds, feeling at ease, immediately wanting to know more about him. "Nice to meet you."

"Ahh, an American."

With a little smile and a twinkle in her eye, Emma replies, "Yes, I'm from California!" Poul grins warmly. "As soon as Americans speak, we Europeans know who you are," he teases gently. "So, what brings you to Vienna?"

"I am an art historian," Emma shares, "and currently I'm writing an article on Klimt's *The Kiss.* What about you—what has brought you here?"

"I am an attorney who tries to find art that was stolen by the Nazis during World War II. I have visited Vienna a number of times."

Emma's eyes widen in surprise. "That's fascinating. What important work. I have always been intrigued by how stolen art is recovered.

I would love to hear more about what you do."

"Yes, I can share," he responds. "But since we are in front of this impressive work, tell me, what does this painting, *The Kiss,* speak to you?"

Talking about a work of art is always difficult for Emma. She much prefers writing about it, which comes naturally. But as an art historian and someone who treasures art in all its expressions, she doesn't want to miss this opportunity to share her thoughts. Shyly, she begins her assessment of this famous work

that has touched so many hearts across sever-
al generations.

"Well, I would say that every time I look at *The Kiss* I am filled with a melting warmth. The lovers literally melt together with no shame. Look at how Klimt depicts them deeply passionate about each other. They hold each other closely, intimately.

"I am intrigued by what they're wearing, the elaborate patterns on their clothing, the nature crowns—one made of flowers, the other made of vines. I lose myself in the details of the piece, from the rectangles and swirls on the man's robe, to the concentric circles on the woman's dress, and on to the abundance of flowers that mirror the lovers' vibrancy."

Now fully invested with no trace of nervousness left, Emma continues, her eyes studying the painting closely.

"There is a tangible energy between the two. They are in complete harmony with one another. Can you feel it?"

Poul gives a gentle nod.

"The entire composition is so luxuriant and

sensual," she proceeds. "The pair embrace at the edge of a patch of colorful wildflowers that accentuate passion, tenderness … he kisses her cheek fondly. She closes her eyes in contentment. This is a timeless representation of a pair perfectly at ease with each other. Klimt has expertly captured two people in a moment of undeniable, blissful love."

Emma ends her eloquent description, not completely sure where her words had come from. They had simply poured from the depths of her soul.

A tangible silence falls upon her and Poul.

Looking from the painting to him, Emma sees tears filling his eyes. He does not try to hide them. Emma does not know it, but this is the very first time in Poul's life that he's experienced an all-encompassing sense of being at one with a painting at Emma's depth.

Looking straight into her eyes, he whispers, "I have never heard one describe *Thee Kiss* with such depth, such genuine passion. Your heart is in your words."

The two stand with eyes locked on one another. Time loses meaning—does a minute pass, or just a few seconds? It doesn't matter.

An unspoken eternity holds them together in that moment, feelings communicating freely in wordless reverie.

Looking away, Emma glances out the window. Reluctantly returning to the present moment, she realizes she has only a short span of daylight left for her next outing.

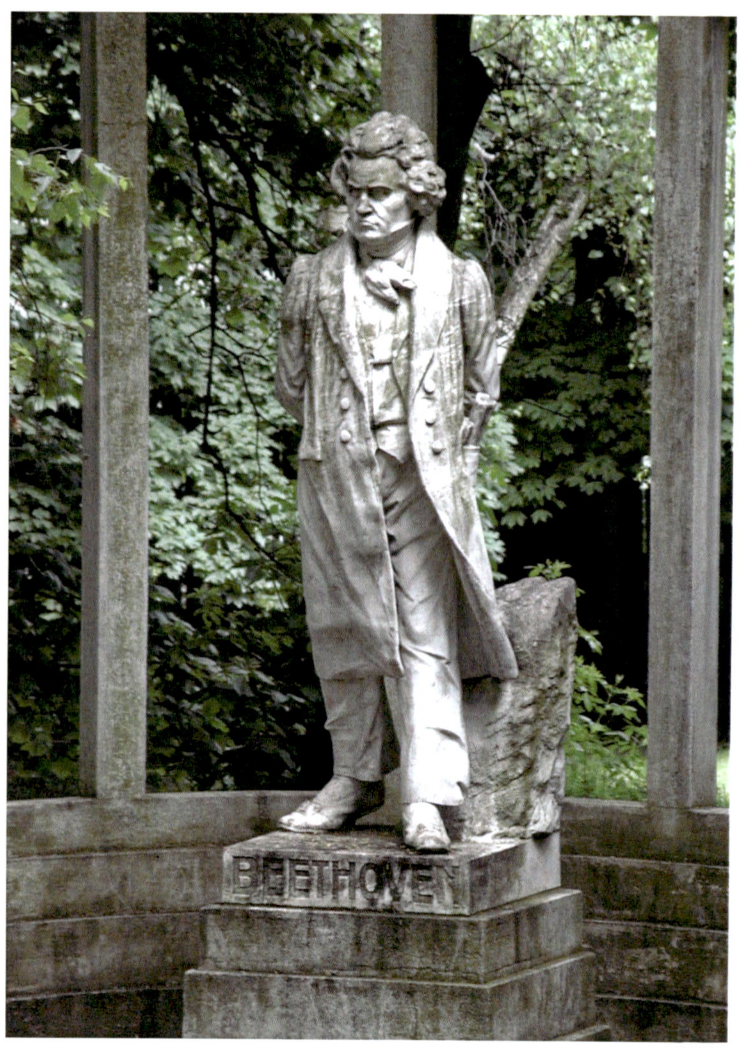

Fritz Hänlein and Robert Weigl. Beethoven Marble Statue. 1910.

Chapter Two

In Beethoven's Footsteps

"I must be going now," she speaks softly, almost apologetically. "It is getting dark. I want to visit Heiligenstadt while there is still daylight."

"What is Heiligenstadt?"

"It's the nineteenth district of Vienna, and my

favorite area of the city," she replies. "Such a charming place. And it's where Beethoven spent a number of summers, each year his deafness growing more profound."

"May I invite myself to accompany you?" Poul asks.

"Oh, of course!" She wonders if he notices her excitement. "I'd be happy to have you join me. I have no doubt you will love Heili-genstadt."

Very quietly Emma and Poul walk out the Bel-vedere into the snowy, silent afternoon, both knowing this one encounter at the museum was, and forever will be, a most serendipitous moment in each of their lives. For both, the experience was transformative—even transcendent. Cold air swirls around them as they stand in a span of silence. A cab arrives. Poul opens the door for Emma. She gets in, and he follows.

"To Heiligenstadt, please," she tells the cab driver.

As they arrive at their destination and leave the cab, Poul takes in his surroundings. "What a charming neighborhood," he says.

Emma smiles. She couldn't agree more. During the early 19th century, Heiligenstadt was a wine-growing village with public baths supplied by a mineral-rich spring said to have healing properties. The region's peacefulness is perfect for contemplation.

The wintry landscape Emma and Poul take in is very different from the lush green trees Beethoven would have experienced during his summer days here, but somehow the composer's timeless essence still echoes through the snowy grounds. Emma and Poul take their time strolling along pathways dusted in snow.

Bundled in winter coats, gloves, and scarves, they leisurely walk along Beethovenweg, the Beethoven Walkway, in the master composer's footsteps. Here, Ludwig had been inspired to write "Scene by the Brook" in his Symphony No. 6—the stream Beethoven walked by daily, hearing nothing but the music in his head.

Emma knows this area well, having walked along the Beethovenweg numerous times listening to the babbling waters, wondering what it must have been like for Beethoven to be immersed in the tranquility of this region. How could it not inspire him, despite his growing torment?

"Can you imagine what it was like for Beethoven to walk by this stream day after day, unable to hear its rippling sounds, yet creating melodious music in his head?"

Poul listens intently to the sound of the stream, still soul-stirring despite being a muffled version of its summertime burbling, and nods in agreement. He's surprised to feel a twinge of sadness as he puts himself in Beethoven's shoes and acknowledges the composer's physical limitations—his humanity. Ordinarily an analytical, left-brain thinker, he wonders what it is about the woman standing next to him that enables him to feel the world through his heart.

They reach the marble statue of Beethoven in Heiligenstadt Park where Emma had stood and reflected many times before. "To me this is the one sculpture made of him that represents his genius as a composer best."

Poul studies the full-body statue. "Go on," he encourages. "Tell me why."

"Notice the faraway look on his face. The sculptor captured his intensity perfectly. The wild hair, his deliberate stride, his hands locked behind his back. Every part of this sculpture fully captures how he must have looked as he visualized his music."

Listening to her words, Poul sees the composer anew—not just as a historical figure, but as a human being who suffered a lifetime, and yet created some of the most glorious music ever made.

When Emma finishes speaking she turns to Poul and realizes that he isn't looking at the statue—his gaze is fixed on her. His eyes speak volumes, revealing he'd never met someone so passionate about art in all its forms … someone so genuinely and innocently real.

"Would you like to explore the Beethoven Museum?" Emma asks.

"Yes, very much," Poul replies.

They walk into an unassuming white stucco building that at one time housed apartments. Today it is a museum that gives visitors an intimate look into Beethoven's life and works.

What makes this museum so unique is not

just the collection of music, photographs, and period artifacts on display, but also, perhaps surprisingly, a letter known as the *Heiligenstädter Testament,* a deep, raw expression of rage Beethoven had written to his brothers, Karl and Johann, in response to his increasing deafness. But the composer never sent this letter. He kept it with his private papers, found only after his death. Despite his sense of despair, Beethoven found the strength to persevere, continuing to write music and even taking it in a new direction.

For my brothers Karl and Johann Beethoven

'*O ye men who think or say that I am malevolent, stubborn or misanthropic, how greatly do ye wrong me...I was compelled early to isolate myself, to live in loneliness, when I at times tried to forget all this.*

Oh how harshly was I repulsed by the doubly sad experience of my bad hearing, and yet it was impossible for me to say to men speak louder, shout, for I am deaf... '*Ah how could I possibly admit such an infirmity in the one sense which should have been more perfect in me than in others, a sense which I once possessed in highest perfection...therefore forgive me when you see me draw back when would gladly mingle with you, my misfortune is double painful because it must lead to my being misunderstood.*

I must live like an exile, if I approach near to people a hot terror seizes upon me, a fear that I may be subjected to the danger of letting my condition be observed... but what a humiliation when one stood beside me and heard a flute in the distance and I heard nothing, or someone heard the shepherd singing and again I heard nothing, such incidents brought me to the verge of despair, but little more and I would have put an end to my life — only art it was that withheld me, ah it seemed impossible to leave the world until I had produced all that I felt called upon me to produce, and so I endured this wretched existence...

Tears swelling in her eyes, Emma whispers, "Heart-wrenching, isn't it?" Poul finds himself speechless, with Emma opening a world in his heart that he never knew existed. Emma points out, "Here is where he wrote some of his most important works." Emma and Poul continue studying the artifacts while listening to the great composer's music playing softly throughout the museum, but neither can get the letter out of their minds.

With their tour of the museum finished, they exit and notice just how dark it is. "We should return to the center of Vienna," Poul advises.

"But I would like to continue our conversation. Would you join me at Café Sacher?"

Emma smiles—a hot latte in this frigid weather sounds inviting, and Café Sacher in the city center is no ordinary coffee shop. An elegant coffeehouse with the most delicious rich chocolates, cakes, and coffee in Vienna, it offers the perfect setting to get to know one another better. "Yes, absolutely!"

In contemplative silence, they call for a taxi.

Chapter Three

The Cafe

Arriving at Café Sacher they escape into blissful warmth, wonderful aromas greeting them. The café's ambiance is lively, jovial, but not overwhelming—an ideal setting for conversation at a table for two by the window.

Emma marvels at how Poul puts her at complete ease. Although they'd just met that day, being with him feels like being reunited with a dear friend she's known for ages. They order coffee and dessert. As she takes in the café's comforting scents and sounds, along with sips of her latte and bites of her cake, she gazes at Poul openly. His eyes smile back.

Is she dreaming this? Being here with this man is so beautiful. So perfect.

Diving into conversation, they lose track of time. Poul learns Emma had been divorced since her early forties, by choice. After her divorce, she'd had two relationships, but sadly both men had died prematurely. "My greatest joys in life are my son, my daughter, and my four grandsons," she tells him, sharing photos of the family that fills her heart. "And my work keeps me busy, enabling me to travel and do what I love."

Poul shares that he doesn't have any children. He is a widower of fifteen years who lost his wife after her long battle with breast cancer.

For both, the idea of dating is too painful. Neither feel their heart can handle the deep loss of a partner again. Since losing his wife, Poul has lived in his brain, immersed in his work. And after her relationship losses, Emma experiences romance through art and music.

A contemplative silence comes over them. No more words on the subject are necessary. They move the conversation to Vienna—their trips to this city over the years, what they love about being here, and the allure that always pulls them back. With their coffee cups and dessert plates now empty, Emma suddenly has the urge to stroll through Vienna's lively streets and take in all the holiday cheer.

Feeling spontaneous she asks Poul, "Would you like to explore more of the city with me?" He breaks into a big smile. "I would be delighted."

Chapter Four

Music in the Streets

They meander down holiday-lit streets with decorated trees and sparkling ornaments everywhere they look in the early night. More and more city lights twinkle on, illuminating windows and streets alike.

Emma and Poul arrive at the 12th-century St. Stephen's Cathedral, Vienna's oldest cathedral and the Mother Church of the city's

Roman Catholic Archdiocese. They study the architecture, noticing the south tower that was once the highest point and most prominent feature of the city. They marvel at the Romanesque and Gothic style of the cathedral, remarking on the ornate patterns on the roofs. Beautiful notes of a lone piano travel to where they stand, emanating from the entrance doors that are propped slightly open. They walk inside to hear the music better.

Quietly Emma and Poul take a seat inside St. Stephen's and listen to the lively, playful sounds of a piano sonata by the great 18th-century Austrian composer, Wolfgang

Amadeus Mozart, now being recreated by a young pianist, a teenage boy in what appears to be a private recital. Emma closes her eyes and bathes in the sweet, lyrical music, feeling it deep in her soul. Time stands still. She feels transported back to her own piano recitals from her youth.

When the music stops they linger a moment before leaving the cathedral. Outside in the dark of night fresh fallen snow sparkles like millions of tiny diamonds.

Poul asks, "What is the connection between the great Mozart and this impressive cathedral?"

"St. Stephen's is the church where Mozart wed, as well as where a small service was held for him after his premature death at the age of thirty-five."

"We must always live life with vigor, breathe in every precious moment," Poul responds pensively, "since we do not know what to-morrow will bring."

Emma nods in complete agreement.

Lost in their own thoughts, neither Emma nor Poul have any idea how far they are walking. Meandering along the streets, they arrive at an area where they feel as if they've stepped back in time. The air is alive with celebration. People are dressed in traditional Alpine attire. Christmas carolers fill the space with the sound of music. There is so much to see and experience—all their senses are being awakened in this festive setting. The delicious aroma of chestnuts roasting, the market stalls brimming with colorful, hand-blown glass ornaments—everywhere they turn it's a sensory delight.

So this is the internationally known Christmas Market!

Emma and Poul giggle as they meander through the market, the largest in Vienna, Christkindlmarkt on the Rathausplatz, in front of City Hall. There is so much to take in. They stop and look at handcrafted toys, from nutcrackers to dollhouses of all shapes and sizes. Children run around with free abandonment.

The two of them peruse row after row of elaborately decorated stalls, some with unique trinkets, others with tempting, one-of-a-kind desserts on display. They sip mulled wine and taste gingerbread as they absorb the cheerful chatter of people all around. The lights, the decorations, the caroling, the festive glow—

they feel warm inside despite the chill in the air. "It is easy to fall in love with Vienna in winter," Poul observes.

They continue to walk down illuminated streets, arm in arm, marveling at it all. They explore charming little alleys, also decorated with sparkling lights, each area overflowing with nostalgic charm.

"What about an ice cream cone?" Poul blurts out unexpectedly.

"Ice cream?" For a second it seems absurd to Emma in this cold, but then again, nothing about this evening is real. In fact, every-

thing is magical. Grinning like a child, Emma

agrees.

They head to Eisslon Tuchlauben, one of the

best ice cream shops in Vienna. Poul orders

a double scoop of coffee-flavored ice cream,

while Emma gets a double scoop of mint

chocolate chip. "It goes well with the holiday

colors," she says with a child-like grin.

Savoring the ice cream, they stroll hand in

hand down more alleyways, not saying a

word, just enjoying each other in the moment.

Soon they come upon an enormous outdoor

ice-skating rink, the famed Wiener Eistraum,
with people of all ages gliding across the
smooth surface.

"Shall we give it a go?" Poul asks.

"Yes, let's!"

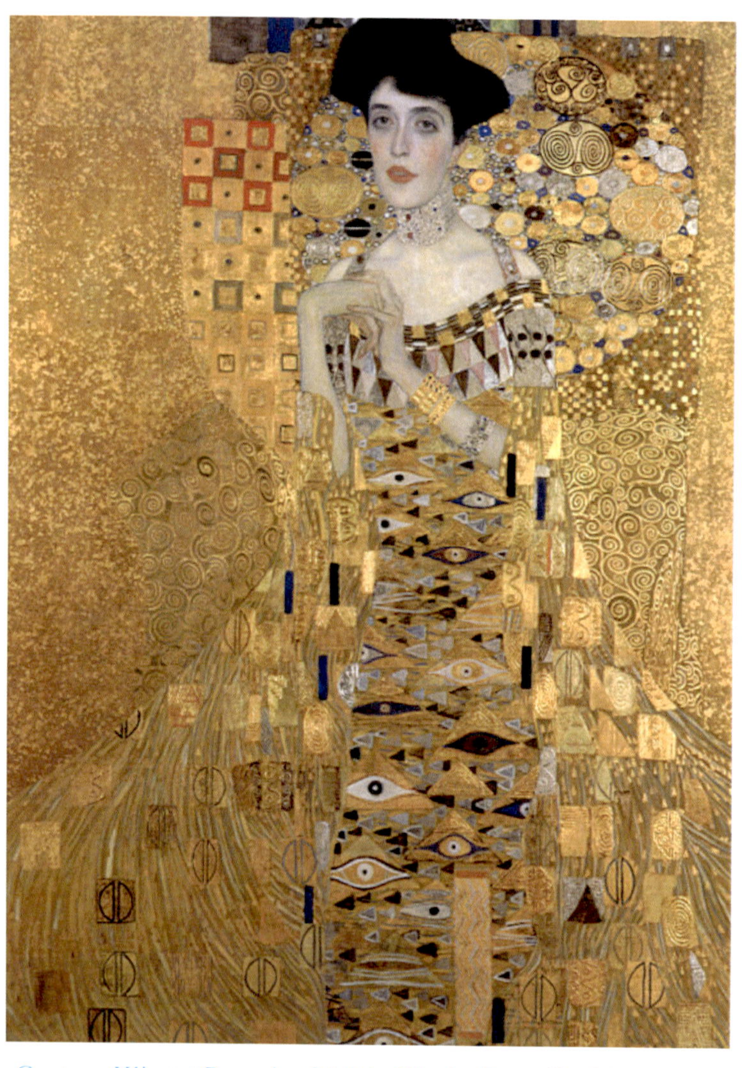

Gustave Klimt. "Portrait of Adele Bloche-Bauer". 1906. oil and
gold leaf on canvas. Neue Galerie. New York

Chapter Five

A Magical Night

As they lace up their rental skates, they feel like children once more.

Emma cautiously steps onto the ice first, with Poul right behind. They laugh as they try to steady themselves. Soon Poul is gliding along, clearly the more accomplished skater. As he turns to skate backward for a short stretch, Emma confides that this is her first time ice skating. "I must tell you, I am not an ice skater. My only experience is roller skating as a child."

"You are doing fine," Poul encourages. "Here, I will guide you."

He glides to her side and takes her by the hand, leading her around the rink. "See? You are doing great!"

"You're too kind!" Emma responds, feeling clumsy but relishing every moment with him.

After much laughter they ease into a relaxed

glide, continuing side by side, hand in hand. Snow begins to fall again, ever so gently, like magic stardust floating down from the endless sky. Smiling children point to the falling snow, reveling at its enchantment. As skaters float past, Poul gently takes Emma by the waist and make their way to the center of the rink.

They pause for a moment, marveling at the gentle snowfall. Poul turns to face Emma. They stare deeply into each other's eyes, holding each other close. He leans in and kisses her, passionately, as they melt into each other like Klimt's lovers. It's a kiss neither wants to end.

Everything around them disappears. Skaters pass by, but the two remain unaware of anyone, anything around them.

Undeniable bliss.

Melting warmth.

Complete harmony.

They gently pull away and stare into one another's eyes in silence, an inner glow emanating from their hearts and growing, encircling them in warm energy.

Lost in an eternal, golden moment of euphoric love, they communicate wordlessly.

With the rink closing soon they must move on. But neither wants this evening to end. As they return their skates and don their shoes, they walk leisurely into the night, arms around each other.

"Perhaps another latte at Café Sacher?" Poul breaks the silence.

"That sounds delightful."

Chapter Six

In Quiet Conversation

Finding a private corner, Emma and Poul order two lattes and one sachertorte to share—chocolate cake with apricot filling, Café Sacher's most famous dessert.

"I've told you a little about what I do as an art historian," Emma begins. "Now I want to hear more about your work. I've read many tragic stories about art theft during the Nazi regime, but I've never had the opportunity to speak with an expert. What's it like being in art theft restitution?"

Poul takes a deep breath and looks out the window, his face growing serious. "Well, retrieving stolen art is difficult, and it is heart-wrenching," he shares. "The heirs of Jewish collectors whose art was stolen by the Nazis face so many challenges."

Emma listens intently, her full attention placed on Poul's words.

"Courts have success and failure working with the families going through the legal system to recover personal works of art. Legal battles between current art owners, claimants, and museums often are intense. Retrieving a work of art can take years."

Poul looks at his coffee, deep in thought, weighing his words carefully.

"The logical part of me, the side the world sees, works well to help claimants go through the necessary but difficult steps to retrieve their art. But my heart hurts at the cruelty and unfairness many people face. It is painful to see the deep disappointment whenever a claimant does not succeed."

Emma is moved by the depth Poul shows. She reaches out and gently touches his hand. "Thank you," he replies, squeezing her hand softly. "Of course, when a case is successful and I see the tears of joy in the rightful owner's eyes, I am overjoyed."

"I would not be able to do the work you do, Poul. My heart would break every time I lost a case. I know you are heartbroken whenever justice fails."

Poul smiles, appreciative of Emma's kindness. A fond memory jolted Emma's mind. "Oh, I remember visiting the Neue Galerie in

New York City in 2016 to see Klimt's painting *Woman in Gold*. It is a portrait of Adele Bloch-Bauer, a Jewish woman and socialite popular in Vienna at the beginning of the 20th century, painted by Gustav Klimt in 1907 in a style very similar to *The Kiss*. Adele was an avid art collector and patron. She had a close relationship with Klimt and was the only person the artist painted twice."

"I know this piece well," says Poul, listening intently.

"During World War II, the Nazis stole this painting from her family's home," she continues. "Eventually it ended up at the Belvedere Museum. In the late 1990s, Adele's niece, Maria Altmann, a Holocaust refugee who had escaped from Austria to America, came forward to claim artwork that had been looted during the war but rightfully belonged to her family. After years of legal battles, she won—in 2004, the U.S. Supreme Court ruled in her favor. Austria returned looted paintings to Maria and other family members. Maria donated *Woman in Gold* to the Neue Gallerie."

"Yes," Poul notes, "this is one of our success stories, thanks to the strength and per-

severance of Maria and her young lawyer,
E. Randol Schoenberg, grandson of the re-
nown Austrian-American composer, Arnold
Schoenberg."

"I am thrilled the painting was returned to
its proper owners," Emma offers. "The painting is absolutely stunning. Adele's gown is
jewel-like, with lustrous gold and silver. Her
delicate, porcelain face and dreamy, faraway
gaze made me want to learn more about her."

"I wish all our cases were as successful as
this one," Poul says softly.

Chapter Seven

Once in a Lifetime

Emma and Poul become quiet as they sit side by side, gazing into each other's eyes. What a day it has been. Each wonders at the serendipity that brought them together in this place at this moment in time.

"Ice skating with you today was magical," Emma says.

Poul smiles. "I will cherish it always. And seeing the gentle snowfall with you, what a joy."

"You know, the first time I see snow in Vienna is always magical," Emma confides. "I love waking up to a winter wonderland. The person who once said that, like kindness, snow beautifies everything it covers, is right. It can take away our sadness, if only for a moment."

"Yes," Poul agrees, "snow is poetic. Nostalgic."

They watch the people walking by. The crowds outside thin out. Soon very few people are seen walking the streets of Vienna.

"I have an early flight back to Copenhagen

tomorrow," Poul shares reluctantly.

"And I have a long flight back to California," Emma responds with tears building up in her eyes.

Their lattes finished, and the café soon closing, Emma and Poul slowly walk outside back into the snow flurries. They stroll a little way, arm in arm. Without a word, they turn and stare deeply into each other's eyes. They embrace and kiss once more—gently, poignantly.

Slowly they let go of each other. Both have

tears in their eyes. With a little nod of know-ingness they turn around, and as the church bells chime at midnight, they walk their sep-arate ways.

Through her tears Emma feels a soft smile forming. She understands why.

For the first time in her life she had experi-enced the mystery of *pure* love, though only for a fleeting moment in time…

* * * * *

One of the greatest gifts in life are the moments that take your breath away... it is my wish you are blessed with many.

-Betty Ann